Vicarious Living in 59 Easy Steps

Vicarious Living in 59 Easy Steps

Jack Seven
and
Pat Pending

FAWCETT COLUMBINE • NEW YORK

To all those who prefer to live
through the media,
To those who wish to learn how to
live through the media,
And to Brian Wilson and Catherine Deneuve,
We Dedicate This Book.

A Fawcett Columbine Book
Published by Ballantine Books

 Published in the United States by Ballantine Books, a division of Random House, Inc., New York, and simultaneously in Canada by Random House of Canada Limited, Toronto.

Library of Congress Catalog Card Number: 85-90588

ISBN: 0-449-90163-7

Cover design by Georgia Morrissey

Manufactured in the United States of America

First Edition: August 1985

10 9 8 7 6 5 4 3 2 1

1. STAY at home most of the time, indoors. This is generally cheaper, easier, safer and less boring than other pursuits.

2. SIMPLIFY your life. Complexity inevitably leads to complications.

3. WATCH a lot of television and try to pick out the mistakes.

4. READ trashy paperbacks about rich, powerful, good-looking people. Imagine you're one of them.

5. MAKE all your time leisure time.

6. DON'T try to create anything original. Remember that it's probably already been done.

7. KEEP a lot of machines around for company.

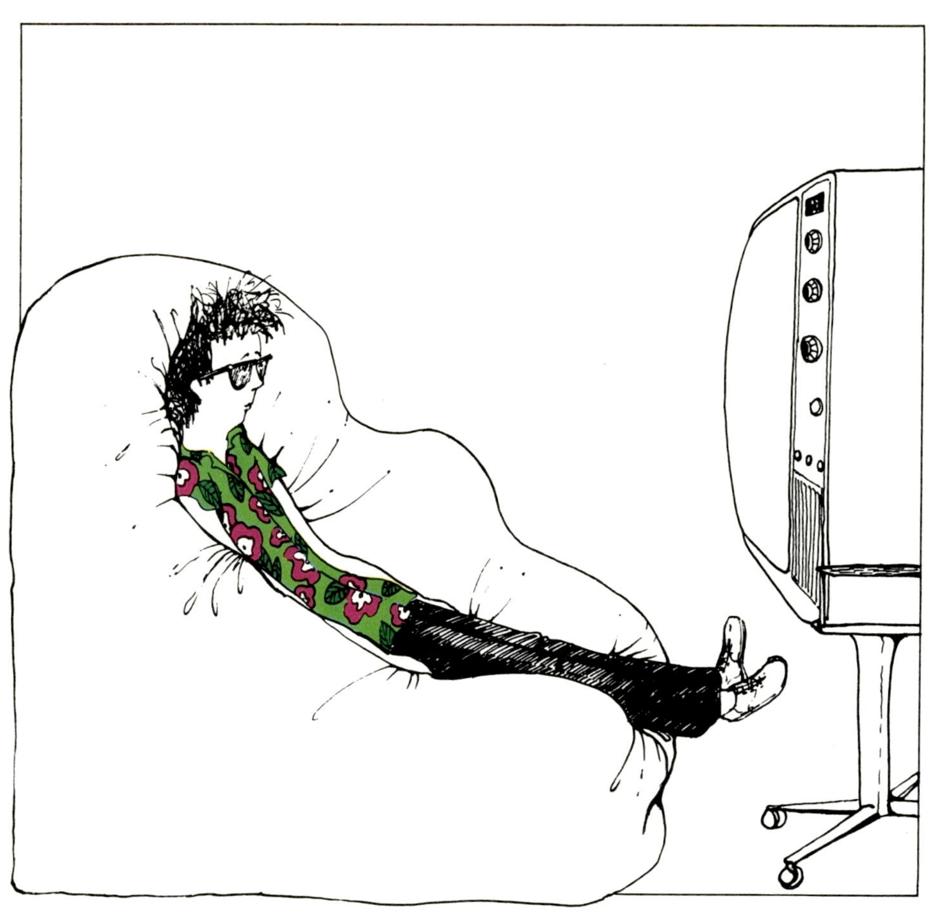

8. TRY to do as little as possible. Remember that activity is a major cause of stress.

9. WEAR sunglasses all the time, especially indoors and at night. This will almost certainly discourage people from trying to communicate with you.

10. DRESS in sneakers and Hawaiian shirts. This will eliminate having to decide what to wear when you get up every morning.

11. GET your reality from television. They usually have a lot of it between 6 and 8 o'clock at night.

12. GET together with your friends at least once a year. The Super Bowl is a good time.

13. TAKE long baths. Reenact the Battle of Midway.

14. **NEVER** watch in person what you can view on video.

15. LIVE your life in a self-contained, insulated, remote, controlled environment.

16. AVOID making sudden changes in your routine.

17. DO whatever you can to avoid working for a living. It is very difficult to try to live vicariously while holding down a steady job.

18. COMMUNICATE with people by playing records on your stereo.

19. DON'T be a conspicuous consumer. Surround yourself with everything you'll ever need and then stop buying forever.

20. WATCH game shows as soon as you wake up. Answer all the questions.

21. TAKE occasional expeditions to department stores to see all the TV's they have on at the same time.

22. EXPERIENCE all your failures vicariously. They hurt a lot less that way.

23. WEAR stereo headphones with some frequency. Listen to a lot of Fleetwood Mac albums.

24. WHEN you visit the real world, always look like a tourist.

25. PRETEND you're a successful Hollywood star sitting out by your swimming pool.

26. SPEND most of your time living in the past or the future. It's usually much more interesting than whatever is happening in the present.

27. DON'T put anything on your schedule that isn't listed in *TV Guide*. Get up after television goes on the air and go to sleep before it signs off.

28. KEEP your ego in check. Never perform for anybody.

29. LISTEN to all the old records in your parents' collection. You might learn a few new clichés.

30. NEVER attend professional sporting events in person. This is too much reality for almost anybody to handle.

31. STAY on an even keel. If you feel yourself starting to become depressed, get up and change the channel.

32. TALK to beatniks, hippies and punks to find out what life was like in the good old days.

33. NEVER answer your front doorbell.

34. SPEND more time in supermarkets than in hospitals. Watch out for anyone wearing a white uniform.

35. PRETEND you don't have any talent and no one will ever ask you to do anything.

36. HAVE an active fantasy life with commercial girls. You only have to see them when they're at their best.

37. HOPE that there is never a blackout.

38. KEEP your opinions and ideas to yourself, if you have any. You can only hope that others will do the same.

39. REMEMBER that you can't possess the images. But you can try.

40. HAVE only long-distance romances.

41. BE more of a voyeur than an exhibitionist. It's a lot harder to make a fool of yourself in the audience than it is onstage.

42. DON'T make behind-the-scenes visits to movie sets, television tapings, or recording studios. It could spoil the illusion.

43. READ advice columns and watch soap operas to make you realize how much better off you are than most people.

44. AVOID contact with the government whenever possible. If they don't know where to find you, they can't come after you.

45. HAVE a lot of heroes like Davy Crockett, Robin Hood, Batman and Clint Eastwood.

46. MAINTAIN an air of detachment about you at all times.

47. TO show your appreciation for all they've done, take an anchorperson to dinner.

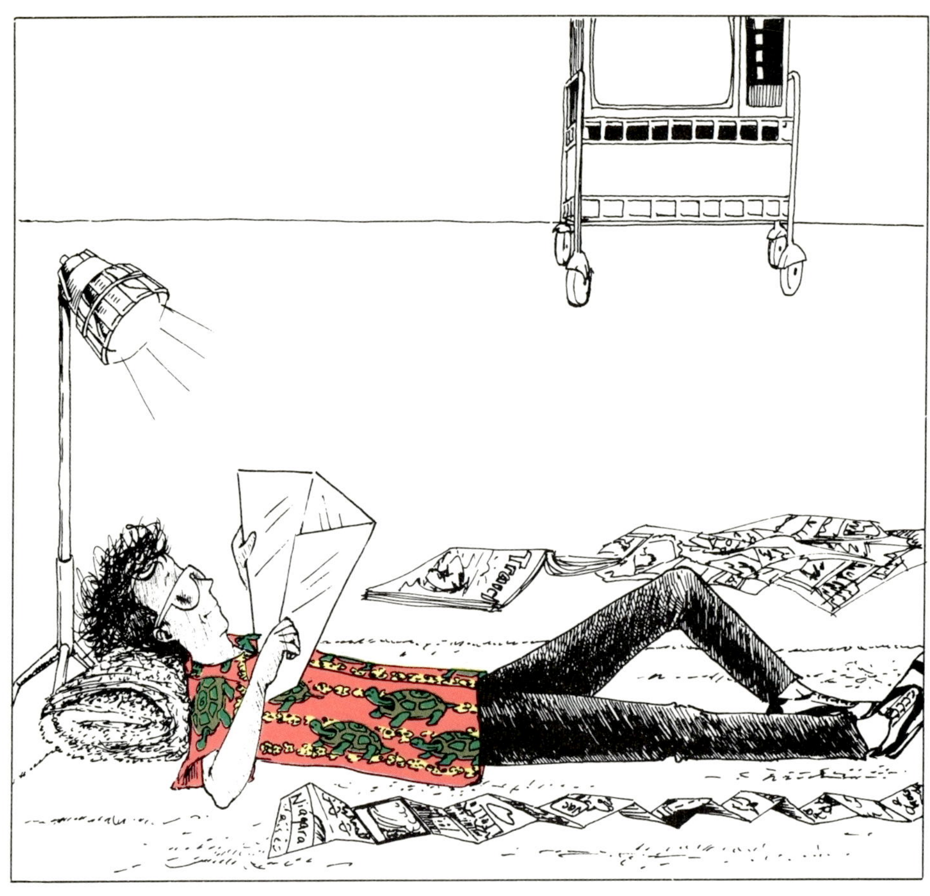

48. TAKE all your vacations vicariously. It always looks much better in the brochures.

49. LEAVE well enough alone.

50. DO things with dolls that you would never consider doing yourself.

51. WISH you could get as many girls as Elvis Presley.

52. RESOLVE not to go to movies in theaters anymore. It's much more vicarious to watch them at home.

53. AVOID anything called "art" or "avant-garde." Let the critics deal with self-expression.

54. DON'T let anybody capture you on film or on tape.

55. PUT off as much as you can until tomorrow.

56. KEEP anything resembling spontaneity or improvisation from creeping into your life. Stick to the rituals, like Johnny Carson.

57. BE decisive in your own home. Maintain control of the channel selector at all times.

58. RELAX – your neighbors are watching the same thing you are.

59. NEVER EVER actually attempt to visit Hawaii in person.